GOD'S
PRESCRIPTION FOR
ADDICTION

THERE HAS NEVER BEEN A
BETTER TIME TO TRANSFORM
YOUR LIFE!

NICK AND CHERYL ELLIOTT

ISBN 978-1-0980-6322-1 (paperback)
ISBN 978-1-0980-6323-8 (digital)

Christian Faith Publishing, Inc.
832 Park Avenue
Meadville, PA 16335
www.christianfaithpublishing.com

Printed in the United States of America

DEDICATION

I would like to dedicate this book to Jesus Christ, my Lord and Savior. I would not have my next breath without Him. He saved me, healed me, and delivered me from darkness. He set me free! It is no longer I that lives, but Christ that lives within me. The same things He did for me, He wants to do for you too! Give Jesus everything you have, and in return, He will give you everything He has for you!

CONTENTS

ACKNOWLEDGMENTS

I would like to thank my loving wife of twenty years, Cheryl (Cherbear). You have been there when I was at my worst. You have seen me like no one else has ever seen me. You know all of my strengths and weaknesses. You have been there for all the ups and downs.

Through it all, you always put God first! You have been the best example of a follower of Jesus that I have ever seen. You have shown me what it is to love unconditionally. You will never know how much you truly mean to me and how much I love you. I want you to know that everything we have gone through has prepared us for where we are right now. God is going to use all of it for His glory!

I want to publicly thank you for your kindness, patience, perseverance, and love. I also want to thank you for our beautiful daughter, Alina, that has many of your wonderful qualities.

Thank you for showing me what God is really like; this world is a better place because you are in it! I love you always and forever!

This book is written with special thanks:

- My beautiful wife, Cheryl (Cherbear)
- My daughter, Alina
- My parents, Mary and Mackie
- Pastor Annette Damico (Mama)
- Pat, Lynnette, and Grace Sullivan

Thank you all for believing in me even when I was at my lowest point. The Lord puts people in your life at the right time and when you need them the most. I thank God for each of you and pray His continued favor and blessings upon your lives. I love you all!

INTRODUCTION

My best friend died at forty-eight years old from alcoholism, and I've watched countless other friends and family members either die or come extremely close to death. I have also abused drugs and alcohol, although I hid it very well. I'm sure many people I know that are reading this right now are surprised.

The world has a twelve-step program and labels you as a drug addict or an alcoholic for your whole life. I am writing this book because I've discovered a one-step program and His name is Jesus. When you surrender your whole life to Him, He will give you a brand new one filled with hope, love, peace, and joy every day.

As I started to write this book, I shared with my wife what I was writing, and she would bring great insight and revelation as to what needed to be said, so I felt it only right to make her the coauthor.

The Holy Spirit has literally guided us and directed us through this process. This is the process that has set me free, and I believe it will do the same for you! The old things will pass away and all things will become new. God is bigger than the addiction in your life!

We have both witnessed the hurt, pain, loss, and trauma caused by addiction. Through this book, our prayer is that we will see the deliverance and restoration of many who have been bound. John 8:36 says, "He who the Son sets Free is Free indeed!"

CHAPTER 1
Enough Is Enough

You have circled this mountain
long enough; turn northward.
—Deuteronomy 2:3

What mountains have you been circling? Drugs, alcohol, pornography? Our heart in writing this book is to see you conquer your mountain. Stories inspire change, but they don't always tell you how to do it.

This book is titled *God's Prescription for Addiction* because you are going to find Him in every chapter! Through God and His Word, you are going to find the answers and the tools needed for you to overcome addiction.

The first step is coming to the point where you say enough is enough! You make the decision you don't want to keep circling the same mountain! It is a place of total surrender where you come to the end of yourself.

Success will require you to be "all in." You will have to put what you want and what you feel aside and let the Lord lead you through this process.

James 1:8 says a double-minded man is unstable in all of his ways. If you move forward and make the decision to commit to this process, you can't go back and say, "Well, I will do this but not that." It just won't work.

You are going to have to surpass the level of darkness that you have allowed in your life with the love of God and the light of His Word.

What we are going to share with you throughout this book is the truth, but it is going to require effort on your part. If you choose to grab hold of it and do what is written in these pages, we have no doubt you will be set free.

If you are honest with yourself, you'll admit that what you've been trying to fill up with is not fulfilling at all and you always need more. It's like taking a drug: you feel peace for a moment, but it's a false peace. It never lasts; there is always a point where you come down and you need more. There is always a need for that next fix, and it never really fulfills you at all. True peace only comes through Jesus Christ.

Do you remember when you were a child in school and they asked you what you wanted to be when you grew up? How many of the kids do you remember raising their hand and saying, "I want to be a drug addict! I want to be an alcoholic! I want to be a prostitute!" The answer is *zero* because nobody was created to be any of those things!

You were created for a great purpose and a divine destiny! You were called to impact the lives of those around you in a positive and powerful way. So why aren't you?

Let me tell you why. You've been listening to lies from the enemy, telling you that you will never amount to anything, your situation is impossible, things are never going to change, the world would be better off without you and there is no hope!

There are a multitude of reasons as to why people get caught up in addiction, but I'm not here to talk about the problem, I'm here to give you the solution.

I have some good news for you! John 8:32 says you will know the truth and the truth will set you *free*!

His name is Jesus! The world doesn't want to hear about Him, governments want to eliminate Him, and the devil doesn't want you to believe He is real, but let me tell you from personal experience that He is real and He is the answer to every problem in your life!

My Transformation
(Nick Elliott)

I was raised in the church by a Spirit-filled mom (Mama Mary). She was always a good mom and loved me, my four brothers, and two sisters no matter what we did wrong. She has always been a good example of how to keep your eyes on Jesus through the storms of life. There was a time in my life I almost died, and with the love of Jesus, she helped bring me back to life. Thank you, Mom, I love you forever!

My dad was a little more reserved and kept those matters of the heart between himself and God. He taught me how to work hard and be consistent. Thank you, Dad, I love you! I am thankful for my parents and would not be where I am today without their love!

I have been married to my lovely wife, Cheryl (Cherbear), for twenty years. We have been through so much together, from bankruptcy to being on the verge of divorce as well as everything in between. She has not left my side and has stood on the Word of God through the storms of life. Thank you, love, for not giving up on me. Cherbear, I love you always and forever!

We have one child, Alina, who is fourteen years old. She is a talented and beautiful young lady who loves God with her whole heart. I am so proud of the choices she makes and how she stands for Jesus. You are the best daughter I could have ever hoped for. I love you, sweetie, always and forever!

To all my brothers and sisters, John, Jay, Joey, Max, Sarah, and Lisa. I love you all and I hope this book inspires you to go for your God-given destiny with every fiber of your being! And no matter how hard it gets, God is with you. Lisa, you can see why I put you last if you look up Matthew 20:16.

I also have to mention my pastor and Italian spiritual mom (Mama Annette). The Lord brought you into my life at the right time and in the right season. You played an intricate part in me surrendering my whole life to Jesus. Thank you for answering the call! Love you, Mama!

Now that I have shared a little about the people in my life who've been the closest to me, let me share with you what transpired on that day in December 2018. My life was forever changed and transformed by my Lord and Savior Jesus Christ. I am a new creation in Christ Jesus, the old things have passed away and all things have become new!

I lived for myself most of my life. I was running from God and the call he placed on my life before the foundations of the world. When things were good, I was good, and when things were bad, I was bad. I always looked good on the outside, but on the inside, I was on an emotional rollercoaster. My life was being controlled by how I felt at any given moment.

Until that cold, sunny December day when I finally decided enough was enough! I got down on my knees in my bedroom and told Jesus, "I am ready to surrender all! I will give you all the bad that is in me. I will follow You every day for the rest of my life. I've heard about You, I've read about You, I've felt Your presence in church, but I want to know You!"

Before I finished the words I was saying, Jesus walked into my room and filled me with a consuming fire that burned out everything I said I would give Him. Moments later as my body was on fire (in a good way) and tears of joy ran down my face, I was flooded with His love! Jesus was right in front of me. He showed me how much He loved me and that He wanted me to share His love with the world. This is the day Nick Elliott died, and Christ the hope of Glory came alive in me.

As I write this book, that was nineteen months ago, and my whole life has changed. Since that day, I've not watched TV or listened to the radio. I read my Bible, talk to Jesus, pray, and have the most awesome relationship with Him every day. This may seem extreme, but I have gotten extreme results! My mind has been renewed by the Word of God! In everything I do, I do it as unto Him. I am filled with His love, peace, and joy no matter what circumstances I face. I pray with people every day and see them get healed, saved, and set free.

God has done such amazing things in my life, and I am thankful every day! I ran 100 mph for the devil, and now I am running 200 mph for Jesus and His Kingdom!

Jesus, I cannot stop thanking you for what you have done in my life. You have made all the dark places light. You are the reason I live and share your love with this lost and dying world every day. I will love You forever and all eternity!

I'd like to give you an opportunity to surrender your life to Jesus. It's the best decision you could ever make! I can tell you from personal experience, His love is unlike any other, and you can trust Him with the deepest parts of your heart. His love never disappoints! Simply pray the following prayer with your whole heart:

Dear Lord Jesus, I know that I am a sinner, and right now, I repent of my sin. I humbly ask for Your forgiveness. I believe You died on the cross for my sins and rose from the dead. I now choose to turn from my sins and invite You to come into my heart as Lord and Savior. I want to love, trust, and follow You for the rest of my days!

If you just prayed this prayer, your name has been written in the Lamb's Book of Life, and all of heaven is rejoicing! This is the best decision you have ever made!

CHAPTER 2
Not My Will, But Thy Will

Luke 22:42 says, "Father, if it is Your will, take this cup away from Me nevertheless not My will, but Yours, be done."

Jesus didn't say, "Father, please take this cup away from Me! I don't feel like doing this right now. I'm young and I have a lot of life to live!" Jesus wasn't concerned about His life, He was concerned about pleasing the Father and doing His will.

There are some people out there that will say, "I'll give my life to God when I'm older," because they want to keep doing what they are doing. They may want to keep drinking and partying or doing drugs, but it's a sobering reality to find that just one more pill or one more line could send them into eternity. Everyone thinks it won't happen to them, but when you play with fire at some point, you will get burned.

Matthew 16:25–26 says, "For whoever desires to save his life will lose it, but whoever loses his life for My sake will find it. For what profit is it to a man if he gains the whole world, and loses his own soul? Or what will a man give in exchange for his soul?" Our flesh and our spirit are constantly in opposition to one another. Your flesh is going to want to continue doing those things that God wants to deliver you from; however, when Jesus becomes the Lord of your life, it is no longer my will but Thy will.

It is time to align yourself with God and His will. How do you do this? By immersing yourself in the Word of God. The Word of God is your standard, if it doesn't line up with His Word, then it is not His will.

"And do not be conformed to this world, but be transformed by the renewing of your mind, that you may prove what is that good and acceptable and perfect will of God" (Romans 12:2).

The first step is continually reading and meditating on the Word so you can know the will of God. Second, you will need to put your trust in Him. Proverbs 3:5–6 says, "Trust in the Lord with all your heart, And lean not on your own understanding; In all your ways acknowledge Him, And He shall direct your paths." Third, is walking it out. Your actions need to line up with what you have been reading and learning. James 1:22–24 says, "But be doers of the word, and not hearers only, deceiving yourselves. For if anyone is a hearer of the word and not a doer, he is like a man observing his natural face in a mirror; for he observes himself, goes away and immediately forgets what kind of man he was."

To be in His will is a choice you have to make every day. Are you going to do what you want to do or what God wants you to do? Let's look at some examples of people in the Bible who said, "Not my will but Thy will be done."

Shadrach, Meshach, and Abed-Nego or as some people might say My-shack, Yo-shack, and a Bungaloo! These were three young men that dared to believe God even in the face of death. In Daniel 3 when King Nebuchadnezzar made a decree that everyone should bow down to the gold image or be thrown into the burning fiery furnace, these young men said no way!

When confronted with death, they answered the king in Daniel 3:16–18 by saying, "O Nebuchadnezzar, we have no need to answer you in this matter. If that is the case, our God who we serve is able to deliver us from the burning fiery furnace, and He will deliver us from your hand, O King. But if not, let it be known to you, O king that we do not serve your gods, nor will we worship the gold image which you have set up."

Are you going to bow down to the idols in your life or are you willing to jump into the burning fiery furnace and meet Jesus face to face? These young men were in for a big surprise! Due to their obedience and open confession of their faith, when the guards looked into the furnace they saw four men loose, no longer bound as they were when they were thrown in the furnace! They were walking in the midst of the fire, and they were not hurt and the form of the fourth was like the Son of God!

God wants to deliver you from your fiery furnace, but you have to be willing to lay down your life. You can walk out of that addiction just like Shadrach, Meshach, and Abed-Nego walked out of the furnace!

A few chapters later in Daniel 6, we find out that the people in our life are not always for us. Daniel was a governor in the king's kingdom and was being promoted, but not everyone was happy for Daniel. The other governors conspired against him, but they could find no fault. They ended up making a proposal to the king that for thirty days, nobody could worship any other God except the king, and if they were caught doing so, they would be thrown into the lion's den. The governors went to the king and told him their proposal and the king agreed and signed a decree with his signet.

After Daniel saw the king sign the decree, he went home, opened the windows, and started to pray out loud.

Guess who was watching? The other governors. They went to tell the king, and the king regretfully told them to throw Daniel into the lion's den.

The king was regretful because he loved Daniel, but he said, "Don't worry, Daniel, your God that you serve day and night will deliver you."

So that night, they threw him into the lion's den. Early in the morning, the king went down to the lion's den and yelled through the door, "Daniel, has your God delivered you?" and Daniel answered, "Yes, oh King, he has!" and the king rejoiced and gave orders to take him out of there. Things didn't go well for the ones who conspired against him. The king ordered them, their wives, and children to be thrown into the lion's den, and they were ripped apart before their bones ever hit the ground.

There are many things we can learn from this, but right now, I want to point out that Daniel loved God more than anything. He trusted God to deliver him and He did! He decided that he was going to be obedient to His will no matter what and not bow down to anything. We come to find out that the lions weren't able to touch him. Staying in the will of God not only brings blessing but protection! God had Daniel's back, and if you stay in God's will, He will have your back too!

Scriptures to Meditate On:

"Not everyone who says to Me, 'Lord, Lord,' shall enter the kingdom of heaven but he who does the will of My Father in heaven" (Matthew 7:21).

"Therefore submit to God. Resist the devil and he will flee from you" (James 4:7).

"I beseech you therefore, brethren, by the mercies of God, that you present your bodies a living sacrifice, holy, acceptable to God, which is your reasonable service. And do not be conformed to this world, but be transformed by the renewing of your mind, that you may prove what is that good and acceptable and perfect will of God" (Romans 12:1–2).

"For I have come down from heaven, not to do My own will, but the will of Him who sent me" (John 6:38).

"Your word is a lamp to my feet And a light to my path" (Psalm 119:105).

"He who finds his life will lose it, and he who loses his life for My sake will find it" (Matthew 10:39).

"Trust in the Lord with all your heart, And lean not on your own understanding; In all your ways acknowledge Him and He shall direct your paths" (Proverbs 3:5–6).

"In everything give thanks; for this is the will of God in Christ Jesus for you" (1 Thessalonians 5:18).

"For this is the will of God, that by doing good you may put to silence the ignorance of foolish men" (1 Peter 2:15).

CHAPTER 3

Change Your Thoughts, Change Your Life!

And be not conformed to this
world, but be transformed by the
renewing of your mind, that you
may prove what is that good and
acceptable and perfect will of God.

—Romans 12:2

Let me start out by saying you are a spirit, you have a soul and you live in a body. Your soul consists of your mind, will, and emotions. In this chapter, we are going to talk about your mind.

Most people run their lives based upon what they think and feel; however, without God, your mind, will, and emotions can lead you into destructive patterns. Everything starts with a thought, thoughts lead to desire, and after desire has conceived, it gives birth to sin (destructive patterns). If you allow yourself to think on anything long enough, at some point, you will eventually act on it, leading to life or death. The choice is yours.

Proverbs 14:12 says there is a way that seems right to a man, but it leads to destruction. Proverbs 23:7 says, "For as he thinks in his heart so is he." If you are going to be effective in eliminating destructive behaviors and cycles, then you need to renew your mind.

How do you do this? By reading, meditating on, and applying the word of God to your life every day. Philippians 4:8 says that we are to think on those things that are pure, lovely, and of a good report. Someone who has not renewed their mind is going to think wrong things such as dwelling on past mistakes or failures. The good news is that when you become a new creation in Christ Jesus, those old mistakes and failures pass away and all things become new!

Immerse yourself in the word of God! Joshua 1:8–9 says, "This Book of the Law shall not depart from your mouth, but you shall meditate in it day and night, that you may observe to do according to all that is written in it. For then you will make your way prosperous, and then you will have good success. Have I not commanded you? Be strong and of good courage; do not be afraid, nor dismayed, for the Lord your God is with you wherever you go." He just told you how to be prosperous and have good success!

He tells you to meditate on the word and then goes on to say, "Do not be afraid or dismayed." Maybe some of the thoughts you struggle with are related to fear and torment. God knows there are going to be times where we may be tempted to fear, but we can fight fear with faith. As you continue in the Word of God, your thinking will change. Instead of responding out of fear, His word will come out of your mouth!

Deuteronomy 31:6 says, "Be strong and of good courage, do not fear or be afraid of them, for the Lord your God, He is the One who goes with you. He will not leave you nor forsake you." Romans 8:31 says, "If God is for us, who can be against us?" Psalm 34:19 says, "Many are the afflictions of the righteous, But the Lord delivers him out of them all."

These are not just words on a page; they are promises God has given to every believer. Grab hold of these promises for yourself because they will cause you to overcome! As you read and meditate on them make them personal. For example, 1 John 4:4 says, "He who is in me is greater than he who is in the world."

The Word of God pours out of me because that is all that I put inside of me. I am fully persuaded that I am who He says I am and I can do what He says I can do. I believe the whole word and nothing but the word, so help me God. My mind is submitted to the mind of Christ and not what I think.

2 Corinthians 10:5 says that we are to cast down arguments and every high thing that exalts itself against the knowledge of God, bringing every thought into captivity to the obedience of Christ. We need to submit our thoughts to God and resist the devil so he flees. When a destructive thought or temptation comes to your mind, you need to open your mouth and speak the Word. You can't battle the enemy of your soul in your mind. When the devil tempted Jesus in the wilderness, He spoke the Word! There is power in what you speak, and we will be talking about that in the next chapter.

That's why it is so important to read your Bible. The Word of God needs to come alive in you! You need to read it from the perspective of what is God saying specifically to me and how can I apply it to my life? When fear comes against you what are you going to say? 2 Timothy 1:7 says, "I have not been given the spirit of fear but of power, love and a sound mind." 1 John 4:18 says, "Perfect love casteth out all fear." If you don't put it in your heart and mind, it's not going to come out!

Ephesians 5:26 says we are washed by the water of the Word. There are times I have scriptures on my phone and TV at the same time. The Word of God is continually before my eyes because I know that my success and freedom depends on my relationship with Him and on my willingness to abide in His word.

I want to point out that you can read the Word and speak the Word but still not truly believe the Word in your heart. There is a difference in saying something versus believing something. How do you get to the point where you actually believe it? You have to continually think upon it. It has to be like Joshua 1:8 where you meditate on it day and night. You will find that if you do this, what you once knew to be in your head will have dropped down into your heart, and that is where the power is—in your belief!

You need to have the conviction in your heart of knowing what you are believing and speaking is the truth. If you don't believe it, nobody else will either, and when the enemy comes knocking at your door with temptation, you better know that what you believe is true.

There is also a difference between knowing the scriptures and knowing Him (Jesus). Jesus is the one that brings the power; if we don't have His spirit living on the inside of us, then it is like having a match with no fire. He is the one that ignites the fire!

Let Jesus ignite you! Let His word come alive inside of you! There is worldly thinking and there is Kingdom thinking. You want to have God's perspective (Kingdom thinking), and the only way to have His perspective is through

His word. As I stated earlier, what you think doesn't matter. What you think needs to be based on what God says.

The Word of God needs to become a mirror or a reflection of your thought process. The more time you spend in His word, the more your decisions will reflect the Kingdom of God. Romans 12:2 says, "And do not be conformed to this world, but be transformed by the renewing of your mind, that you may prove what is that good and acceptable and perfect will of God."

This is how you change your thoughts to change your life!

Scriptures to Meditate On:

> "For God has not given us a spirit of fear, but of power and of love and of a sound mind" (2 Timothy 1:7).

> "For though we walk in the flesh, we do not war according to the flesh. For the weapons of our warfare are not carnal but mighty in God for pulling down strongholds, casting down arguments and every high thing that exalts itself against the knowledge of God, bringing every

thought into captivity to the obedience of Christ" (2 Corinthians 10:3–5).

"And do not be conformed to this world, but be transformed by the renewing of your mind, that you may prove what is that good and acceptable and perfect will of God" (Romans 12:2).

"Finally, brethren, whatever things are true, whatever things are noble, whatever things are just, whatever things are pure, whatever things are lovely, whatever things are of good report, if there is any virtue and if there is anything praiseworthy—meditate on these things" (Philippians 4:8).

"And be renewed in the spirit of your mind, and that you put on the new man which was created according to God, in true righteousness and holiness" (Ephesians 4:23–24).

"Set your mind on things above, not on things on the earth" (Colossians 3:2).

"For this is the covenant that I will make with the house of Israel after those days, says the Lord: I will put My laws in their mind and write them on their hearts; and I will be their God, and they shall be My people" (Hebrews 8:10).

"You will keep him in perfect peace, Whose mind is stayed on You, Because he trusts in You" (Isaiah 26:3).

CHAPTER 4

The Old Man Is Dead!

For all that is in the world—the
lust of the flesh, the lust of the
eyes, and the pride of life—is not
of the Father but is of the world.
—1 John 2:16

And those who are Christ's have crucified
the flesh with its passions and desires.
—Galatians 5:24

You have to be able to say no to the desires of the flesh if
you want to be successful at having a new life.

There are four things that will determine your success!

1. What you watch
2. What you read

3. What you listen to
4. Who you spend your time with

If you really want a new life, you will need to change all of the above. If you have been addicted to pornography, you will have to close every door that you've opened, whether that be a magazine, the internet, your phone, etc. If you truly want to be free, then you will also need to be accountable. There needs to be safeguards in place that will not allow you to do what you've done before. Accountability plays a huge part.

Let me explain what I mean by safeguards. You can block websites, you can give a close friend or spouse access to everything that you view on your phone or computer, or you can call someone that can support and encourage you when you are struggling with temptation.

Pride will tell you, "No, I got this, I don't need any help!" but I'm going to tell you, "No, you don't got this and you do need help!" If you are going to break free, you need to humble yourself and acknowledge that you can't do this in your own strength. The devil likes to keep things in darkness, but God desires to bring it to the light. It can be humbling to admit you need help, but the Bible says God gives grace to the humble and opposes the proud.

Remember, it may be hard at first, but the more time that goes by, the easier it becomes. Don't get me wrong, the devil is a liar, and as soon as you commit to getting this out of your life forever, the temptations will start coming; this will absolutely happen, and I'll tell you why. The devil doesn't want you free. He wants to keep you on a chain. He is shaking in his boots because the day you find out who you really are in God is the day he loses control over you!

We need to go to God first in everything, but it is also very important to have people in your life that support you and your desire to be free.

Which brings me to my next point, you may need to let some people go! If it's someone that is doing the very thing that you are breaking free from or they feel it is acceptable behavior, they can no longer be part of your life, even if it's a family member. You may think this is extreme, but what price are you willing to pay to be free? You need to sit down and count the cost.

I'm going to tell you right now that you will never get free hanging around with the same people that are doing the same things as you were. There is power in agreement, and by letting those people go, you are essentially breaking agreement with the bondage.

You may say, what if they want to be free too? My answer to you would be that they need to find someone to be accountable to as well and do exactly what you are doing on their own.

The last point I want to address is what you allow in your ear gate. If you struggle with drugs and alcohol and you continue to listen to songs that encourage doing those things, then you are defeating the purpose. If you find yourself in conversations where coworkers are talking about going to the bar or a party, you will have to excuse yourself. You don't want to put yourself in a vulnerable place, and you don't want to give the devil any opportunity to get you off track.

I certainly don't want to give the devil any credit, but at the same time, I don't want you to be ignorant of his tactics. He knows all of your weaknesses and he will use them against you, but if you give it to God, where you once were weak, He will make you strong!

Please take this to heart. I'm speaking from experience, and if you give the devil an inch, he will take a mile. The good news is that the only power he has is the power you give him.

Looking at things from a worldly perspective can be overwhelming especially if you are looking at all of the problems and what is going wrong, but this is the hope we have in Jesus! James 1:2–4 says, "My brethren count it all joy when you fall into various trials, knowing that the testing of your faith produces patience. But let patience have its perfect work, that you may be perfect and complete, lacking nothing."

When was the last time you counted it all joy when you were going through some type of problem or difficult situation? Probably never, and that is because the world doesn't think that way.

God will even use our problems for our good if we trust Him, but we have to be willing to die to ourselves. You have the ability to choose how you are going to respond to any given situation, and believe it or not, it is possible to praise Him in everything! We have to see things from His perspective.

Galatians 2:20 says, "I have been crucified with Christ; it is no longer I who live, but Christ lives in me; and the life which I now live in the flesh I live by faith in the Son of God, who loved me and gave Himself for me."

If the old man is dead, there shouldn't be any whining or complaining. Have you ever heard a dead man complain? I haven't.

Let Christ live in you, the hope of glory! We should be responding to problems according to our new nature, not the old one. If you are dealing with stress or pressure, you don't run to heroin, you run to God. You can overcome through Him. It's time to crucify your fleshly desires and submit to God. It's time to start doing what is right and not what you feel like doing. Don't let your flesh rule your life! Start to rise up in your spirit man and let your flesh know it's not in control anymore! Remind yourself, the old man is dead!

Scriptures to Meditate On:

"That you put off, concerning your former conduct, the old man which grows corrupt according to the deceitful lusts, and be renewed in the spirit of your mind, and that you put on the new man which was created according to God, in true righteousness and holiness" (Ephesians 4: 22–27).

"And those who are Christ's have crucified the flesh with its passions and desires. If we live in the Spirit, let us also walk in the Spirit" (Galatians 5:24).

"But put on the Lord Jesus Christ, and make no provision for the flesh, to fulfill its lusts" (Romans 13:14).

"For the flesh lusts against the Spirit, and the Spirit against the flesh; and these are contrary to one another, so that you do not do the things that you wish. But if you are led by the Spirit, you are not under the law" (Galatians 5:17–18).

"For those who live according to the flesh set their minds on the things of the flesh, but those who live according to the Spirit, the things of the Spirit. For to be carnally minded is death, but to be spiritually minded is life and peace. Because the carnal mind is enmity against God, for it is not subject to the law of God, nor indeed can be. So then those who are in the flesh cannot please God. But you are not in the flesh but in the Spirit, if indeed the Spirit of God dwells in you. Now if anyone does not have the Spirit of Christ he is not His" (Romans 8:5–9).

"For he who sows to his flesh will of the flesh reap corruption, but he who sows to the Spirit will of the Spirit reap everlasting life" (Galatians 6:8).

"For if you live according to the flesh you will die; but if by the Spirit you put to death the deeds of the body, you will live. For as many as are led by the Spirit of God, these are the sons of God" (Romans 8:13–14).

CHAPTER 5
The Spirit-Led Life

For those who are led by the Spirit
of God are the sons of God.
—Romans 8:14

What is the fruit of a spirit-led life? Galatians 5:22–23 says, "But the fruit of the Spirit is love, joy, peace, longsuffering, kindness, goodness, faithfulness, gentleness, self-control."

What are the works of the flesh? Galatians 5:19–21 says, "Now the works of the flesh are evident, which are adultery, fornication, uncleanness, lewdness, idolatry, sorcery, hatred, contentions, jealousies, outbursts of wrath, selfish ambitions, dissensions, heresies, envy, murders, drunkenness, revelries and the like; of which I tell you beforehand, just as I also told you in time past, that those who practice such things will not inherit the kingdom of God."

Take a moment to evaluate your own life. Are you experiencing the fruit of the spirit or the works of the flesh?

When you make Jesus Christ the Lord of your life, Galatians 2:20 says it is no longer you that lives but Christ that lives within you. Your life needs to be yielded to the Spirit of God. We bear the fruit of the Spirit when we remain in Him. John 15:4–5 says, "Abide in Me, and I in you. As the branch cannot bear fruit of itself, unless it abides in the vine, neither can you, unless you abide in Me."

How do we abide in Him? Through prayer, reading, and meditating on the Word, spending time in His presence, praising Him, thanking Him, and being around other strong Christians.

Leading a spirit-led life means we need to allow our spirit man to be in control. How do you know if your spirit man is in control? You can tell by the fruit of your life! If you are constantly giving your flesh what it wants, then it is clearly in control, but if you are able to crucify your flesh and say no to the things you need to say no to, then you are getting stronger in your spirit man. The goal is to have your spirit man ruling over your flesh. Self-control is one of the fruits of the Spirit.

Love is another fruit of the spirit; in fact, I would encourage you to read 1 Corinthians 13. The entire chapter will tell you what love is, and this is so important because many of us struggle with bitterness, resentment, and unforgiveness in our hearts. Love doesn't hold on to offense, love forgives. Have you ever heard the saying, "Unforgiveness is like drinking poison and waiting for the other person to die"?

There is a story in Matthew 18 about an unforgiving servant. There was a king who was settling accounts, and one of the servants was not able to pay. The master commanded he be sold, with his wife and children and all that he had, and that payment be made, but the servant fell down before him, asking for patience and telling him he would pay him all. The master was moved with compassion, released him, and forgave the debt. However, that same man that was forgiven was given an opportunity to extend forgiveness to a fellow servant, but he wouldn't. The master found out, was angry, and delivered him to the torturers until he paid all that was due to him.

This is an extreme example, but it is the truth. People that can't forgive aren't free. What is holding you back from forgiveness? Hurt, pain, pride? God loves and forgives each one of us when we come to Him and repent. He expects us to extend that same love and forgiveness to others whether we feel they deserve it or not. Forgiveness isn't just for the other person, it's for you too! You don't have to be best friends with the person you forgive, but forgiveness brings a release that will enable YOU to move forward in the Spirit.

We have all been hurt at some point whether it is by friends, parents, relatives, or even strangers. It could be anyone. Many of us have experienced trauma, pain, loss, and disappointment. I would like to take a moment and pray for you to experience God's love in a powerful way.

Father, in the name of Jesus, I pray that you would experience the love of God in such a deep and profound way that you would never question it ever again. Father, touch every part of their hearts so very deeply, every hurt, every wound, every disappointment, every wrong word spoken over them to attempt to throw off their destiny and make them believe something about themselves that isn't true. Father, show them how much they are loved and accepted in You. I pray that Your love would begin to flow on the inside of them like a healing river washing away all trauma, rejection, pain, fear, doubt, or unbelief they've ever known in Jesus's Name, Amen!

Ephesians 3:19 says, "To know the love of Christ *which passes knowledge*; that you may be filled with all the fullness of God." It's not enough to know about His love, it's about knowing Him, He is love.

God is so gracious, He loves us so much! When we repent and turn from something, He is ready to forgive us. You don't have to receive condemnation. You don't have to punish yourself for days, weeks, months, and years. It is under the blood of Jesus and your sins are forgiven! Not only does God forgive us when we repent but He forgets! Hebrews 8:12 says, "For I will be merciful to their unrighteousness, and their sins and their lawless deeds I will remember no more."

You need to forget too! Don't keep replaying it in your head. You can't go back to the past and change anything. There is no sense wasting time and energy thinking about what you could've or should've done. God doesn't live in the past and neither should you. Today is a new day! Live, love, and let go, so you can keep moving forward to your destiny!

The last fruit of the Spirit I'd like to talk about is peace. Many people don't have peace in the world we live in today. They are on drugs of all kinds, including anxiety medications and antidepressants. Jesus said in John 16:33, "These things I have spoken unto you, that in me ye might have peace. In the world you shall have tribulation; but be of good cheer; I have overcome the world." This is great news! Jesus overcame the world and everything in it, so that through Him, you can overcome too. As you learn to abide in Him, you can have the peace that passes all understanding!

His peace doesn't make sense! It isn't based on your circumstances and what is happening in the world, it is based on His kingdom. Hebrews 12:28 says we have received a kingdom which cannot be shaken. This means, it doesn't matter what is going on around you. What matters is who and what is on the inside of you! If you are abiding in Him and His word, then His kingdom dwells within you and it cannot be shaken.

Matthew 7:24–27 says, "Therefore whoever hears these sayings of Mine, and does them, I will liken him to a wise man who built his house on the rock; and the rain descended, the floods came, and the winds blew and beat on that house; and it did not fall, for it was founded on the rock. But everyone who hears these sayings of Mine, and does not do them, will be like a foolish man who built his house on the sand: and the rain descended, the floods came, and the winds blew and beat on that house; and it fell. And great was its fall."

Stay in His Word and abide in Him. Start building the Kingdom on the inside of you so that when the storms of life come you aren't shaken!

God desires for you to lead a spirit-led life so you can enjoy all the fruits of the spirit in your life too!

Scriptures to Meditate On:

"For whatever is born of God is victorious over the world; and this is the victory that conquers the world, even our faith" (1 John 5:4).

"For I always pray to the God of our Lord Jesus Christ, the Father of glory, that He may grant you the spirit of wisdom and revelation in the knowledge of Him, the eyes of your understanding being enlightened; that you may know what is the hope of His calling, what are the riches of the glory of His inheritance in the saints, and what is the exceeding greatness of His power toward us who believe" (Ephesians 1:17–19).

"Let us therefore come boldly to the throne of grace, that we may obtain mercy and find grace to help in time of need" (Hebrews 4:16).

"Draw near to God and He will draw near to you. Cleanse your hands, you sinners; and purify your hearts, you double-minded" (James 4:8).

"Abide in Me, and I in you. As the branch cannot bear fruit of itself, unless it abides in the vine, neither can you, unless you abide in me. I am the vine, you are the branches. He who abides in Me, and I in him, bears much fruit; for without Me you can do nothing" (John 15:4–5).

"So Jesus answered and said to them, 'Assuredly, I say to you, if you have faith and do not doubt, you will not only do what was done to the fig tree, but also if you say to this mountain, 'Be removed and cast into the sea,' it will be done. And whatever things you ask in prayer, believing, you will receive'" (Matthew 21:21–22).

"Therefore we also, since we are surrounded by so great a cloud of witnesses, let us lay aside every weight, and the sin which so easily ensnares us, and let us run with endurance the race that is set before us" (Hebrews 12:1).

"I beseech you therefore, brethren, by the mercies of God, that you present your bodies a living sacrifice, holy, acceptable to God, which is your reasonable service" (Romans 12:1).

"And when he brings out his own sheep, he goes before them, and the sheep follow him, for they know his voice" (John 10:4).

CHAPTER 6
Say What?

For by your words you will be
justified, and by your words
you will be condemned.
                —Matthew 12:37

Genesis chapters 1 and 2 talk about the history of creation, and I would encourage you to read it for yourself. You will find that everything was created through God's spoken word. Hebrews 1:3 says He upholds all things by the word of His power. Since you and I are created in His image and likeness, our words have power as well.

I had a close friend that died several years ago from addiction. He would always say he was old, fat, and ugly. It was really sad because this man had a lot to offer. He was smart, funny, and very generous. He was also wealthy and had the potential to do great things!

I bring this up because I'd like to ask you what you are speaking about yourself? What are you speaking over your life?

Luke 6:45 says, "A good man out of the good treasure of his heart brings forth good; and an evil man out of the evil treasure of his heart brings forth evil. For out of the abundance of the heart his mouth speaks." What do you believe? What are you convinced of? Because what you believe will come out of your mouth.

God doesn't want us to think bad thoughts about ourselves. His thoughts towards us are only good. Jeremiah 29:11 says, "For I know the thoughts that I think toward you, says the Lord, thoughts of peace and not of evil, to give you a future and a hope."

Do you remember when we talked about what we think on? Do you remember me saying that if you think on something long enough, it will drop down into your heart and become part of your belief system? This is why it is so important to take your thoughts captive. You choose what you will think and what you won't. You choose if you want success or failure. Good or bad. You choose if you see yourself as beautiful or ugly.

The good news is that if you have been speaking wrong things, you can turn it around right now! Just say, "Father, in the name of Jesus, I repent for the way I've been seeing myself and the way I've been speaking about myself.

I repent for any negative words I've said about my life or anyone else's life. I ask for your forgiveness, and starting today, I'm only going to speak those things that you would have me to speak!"

"I am a new creation in Christ Jesus, the old things have passed away, and all things have become new. I am the head and not the tail. I am above only and not beneath. I am blessed coming in and blessed going out! I am chosen, loved, redeemed, accepted, forgiven, and blessed! I am more than a conqueror, and I can do all things through Christ Jesus who strengthens me! No weapon that is formed against me shall prosper, but every tongue that rises against me in judgment, I shall show to be in the wrong."

These are the things you need to start saying about yourself every day. I would even recommend looking in the mirror when you say them because you need to see yourself this way. This is who you are!

Romans 4:17 says we are to call those things that are not as though they are. You need to keep speaking those things that are not as though they were until they are! So if you don't believe you are the righteousness of God in Christ Jesus, then you need to keep on saying it and meditating on it until you believe you are!

Hebrews 4:12 says, "For the word of God is living and powerful, and sharper than any two-edged sword, piercing even to the division of soul and spirit, and of joints and marrow, and is a discerner of the thoughts and intents of the heart."

God's word separates truth from lies. It enables you to recognize what is of God and what is not. So the next time the devil tries to bring his lies and deceptions let God's word come out of your mouth so powerfully that hell starts to tremble! It's time for you to pick up your sword (God's word) and use it!

Scriptures to Meditate On:

> "So shall My word be that goes forth from My mouth; It shall not return to Me void, But it shall accomplish what I please, And it shall prosper in the thing for which I sent it" (Isaiah 55:11).

> "Thou shalt also decree a thing, and it shall be established unto thee: and the light shall shine upon thy ways" (Job 22:28).

> "Let the words of my mouth and the meditation of my heart Be acceptable in Your sight, O Lord, my strength and my Redeemer" (Psalm 19:14).

"A soft answer turns away wrath, But a harsh word stirs up anger" (Proverbs 15:1).

"In the multitude of words sin is not lacking, But he who restrains his lips is wise" (Proverbs 10:19).

"Set a guard, O Lord, over my mouth; Keep watch over the door of my lips" (Psalm 141:3).

"Death and life are in the power of the tongue, And those who love it will eat its fruit" (Proverbs 18:21).

"He who would love life And see good days, Let him refrain his tongue from evil, And his lips from speaking deceit" (1 Peter 3:10).

CHAPTER 7

Identity

The worldview looks at someone as a drug addict or an alcoholic. I want to make it very clear to you that God does not see you in that way. He sees you the way He created you. He sees your true identity, and that is how He wants you to see yourself.

I want to share with you what Jesus did on the cross and the events that led up to it. Imagine being in a room filled with people that want to kill you. He was spit on, punched in the face, and beaten beyond recognition even before He went to the cross. He was belittled, demeaned, and degraded by those around him.

On the day of his crucifixion, he was forced to carry the cross on his shoulders while ripped apart and bleeding. He was so weak that he couldn't carry it anymore, so a man in the crowd had to carry it for him the rest of the way. All of his disciples were scattered, watching in the distance. He was all alone.

Once they get to the top of Golgatha, they proceed to take large metal stakes and drive them through his hands and feet to fasten him to the cross. He hung there for more than six hours. He bore every sin on that cross. Anything in your past, present, or future. He paid for it all. It was at this point the one with no sin became sin. He was unrecognizable to man so that our true identity would now be recognized by the Father through Him. What this means for you and I is that we are no longer identified by what we have done or by what happened to us. We are now redeemed by the blood of the lamb and our identity is in Christ alone.

It's time to let God define you. It is time for you to separate what you did from who you are. It is time to let His word and His spirit transform your life. I don't know what your childhood was like or what trauma or abuse you may have endured. What I do know is that as you put your focus on Jesus and allow Him and His word into those areas, He can and will heal you. Don't let what happened to you define you. It doesn't matter what anyone else says or thinks about you! Don't let anything define you except His Word. Your true identity is that you are a child of God and He loves you!

I pray that God opens the eyes of your understanding in such a way that you would see every lie exposed.

Understanding who you are in Christ is the devil's worst fear because when you finally realize who you really are, all of your chains will be broken!

Scriptures to Meditate On:

"I am accepted" (Ephesians 1:6).

"I am the head and not the tail, above only and not beneath" (Deuteronomy 28:13).

"I am blessed coming in and blessed going out" (Deuteronomy 28:6).

"I can do all things through Christ Jesus who strengthens me!" (Philippians 4:13).

"I am more than a conqueror through Him who loves me" (Romans 8:37).

"I have the mind of Christ" (1 Corinthians 2:16).

"I am redeemed from the curse which includes sin, sickness and poverty" (Galatians 3:13).

"My body is a temple of the Holy Spirit" (1 Corinthians 6:19).

"Greater is He that lives in me than He that is in this world" (1 John 4:4).

"I am the righteousness of God in Christ Jesus" (2 Corinthians 5:21).

"I am a new creation in Christ; old things in my life have passed away and all things have become new!" (2 Corinthians 5:17).

"I am a chosen" (1 Peter 2:9).

"Blessed be the God and Father of our Lord Jesus Christ, who has blessed me with every spiritual blessing in the heavenly places in Christ" (Ephesians 1:3).

"God knows the thoughts He thinks towards me, thoughts of peace and not of evil, to give me a future and a hope" (Jeremiah 29:11).

"I am joined to the Lord and I am one spirit with Him" (1 Corinthians 6:17).

"Behold what manner of love the Father has bestowed on me, that I should be called a child of God!" (1 John 3:1).

"I am seated in heavenly places with Christ Jesus" (Ephesians 2:6).

"I have been crucified with Christ; it is no longer I who live, but Christ lives in me; and the life which I now live in the flesh I live by faith in the son of God, who loved me and gave Himself for me" (Galatians 2:20).

"I will praise You, for I am fearfully and wonderfully made" (Psalm 139:14).

CHAPTER 8
A Call to Action

You've received the steps to freedom, and now it's time to put your faith into action. God has truly transformed my life through this process, and He will do the same for you!

The first step is coming to the end of yourself—total surrender! You are finally to the point where you are willing to do whatever it takes to be free.

Next, you will need to submit your will to God. It is no longer you that lives, but He that lives in you! Submit your thoughts, plans, desires, hopes, dreams—everything. He won't disappoint you!

The third step is renewing your mind. This is a major key in transforming your life! Immerse yourself in the Word of God. Read it, meditate on it, and most importantly, get to know Him through it!

Next remind yourself that the old man is dead! You aren't going to do what you used to do. Crucify your flesh.

Don't give it what it wants. It will kick and scream, but that's okay because anything you starve will eventually die. Pay attention to what you watch, read, listen to, and who you spend your time with. These things will determine your success!

Pay attention to the fruit of your life. Are you seeing the fruit of the spirit? Maybe you made a mistake or experienced a setback. That doesn't mean you failed, just repent, turn from it, and keep moving forward. Learn to forgive yourself, don't waste time in shame. Remember when you repent and ask for God's forgiveness, He will not only forgive you but forget all about it. You need to forget too! Make sure you spend time in His presence, praying and praising Him. Get connected to a spirit-filled church and people who are like minded to help you lead a spirit-led life.

It is going to cost you something, but the reward will far surpass what you have left behind. I promise!

Don't forget to speak God's word over your life! His promises are yes and Amen, and they belong to you! Don't give up. Keep speaking those things that are not as though they are until you see them manifest in your life!

Finally, know who you are in Christ. Don't allow *anything* to define you except Him and His word!

It may take time, but let me encourage you! You are building spiritual strength and stamina. You are building your life on a foundation that cannot be shaken because it is built upon the Word of God.

As you immerse yourself in the Word of God and do those things I've outlined for you to do, you will find out that you aren't the same person! You aren't a drug addict, you aren't a prostitute, you aren't an alcoholic...you are a child of God!

It's time for you to fulfill your destiny. It's time for you to rise up out of the ashes. It's time for you to believe who He says you are and do what He says you can do. It's time to live an abundant life for who the Son sets free is free indeed!

CPSIA information can be obtained
at www.ICGtesting.com
Printed in the USA
FSHW010749040121